The One Armed Manager

MORCQX

ACKNOWLEDGMENTS

Cover design, lay-out & illustrations by Sander van Bergen
sander.v.bergen@gmail.com

Translation: Stuart Clarke

One Armed Manager

* Also available as an eBook on Amazon-Kindle
* Original (Dutch) title: *De One Armed Manager* (2014)
(ISBN-10: 1500294039 / ISBN-13: 978-1500294038) NL/BE

**This concise booklet might turn out to be the best gift
you could ever give to your boss!
And not just for your boss……**

SPECIAL THANKS TO

all managers -good and bad- I met during my entire career
all the teams and talents I had the privilege to work with up till now
everyone else who ever inspired me on my journey through
management-land

M. Morcqx - m.morcqx@gmail.com

One Armed Manager

The One Armed Manager

(Keep one hand in your pocket)

The art of managing in a nutshell

PREFACE

The term "one armed manager" refers to the fact that most managers 'over manage', in other words they do far more than required in order to be effective, interfere with ancillary matters and details that should be delegated, losing themselves in daily delusion.

In short, they no longer manage, but let themselves be managed by trivial coincidences and suddenly occurring crises. They tread on their own (and also their employees) toes.

This starting point forms the essence for the lifeline running through this booklet. The advice is therefore firstly to take your foot off the accelerator! Stick one hand in your pocket. Less can be more and better at the same time. In management jargon: creating a win-win situation.

ACCOUNTABILITY

Many hundreds, if not thousands of books for managers have been written and published, many of which do contribute towards a more meaningful field of knowledge for managers in their field of expertise. In this book I just want to briefly - but still in depth(!)- highlight what the basics of being a manager are, showing what is the inevitable foundation. Where it all begins. With yourself. You yourself as a manager. With no preconceptions, concise and to the point, clear and simple, almost playful.....

My advise is to consult the abovementioned trade literature, especially all the hard skills (aspects of knowledge) for the specialized field (yes it is specialized!) in which you find yourself, letting me take the liberty of confining myself to the so called "soft skills" (aspects of personality, these however are more often than not far from soft). Putting them as it were in a nutshell. Not because I feel obliged to add something, more the need to take the essential core from the footlights and place it in the spotlights.

This is what this script is about. A handy book "something to have around". Enormously concise ensuring that for even those with no openings in their diary no obstacle will be posed not to allow reading time. On the contrary. An appeal out of pure love for this field, whilst leaving out any and all unnecessary frills, concentrating simply on giving essential lessons showing starting points in order to be able to take a close look at yourself, the (busy) manager. For all those moments when you just do not have anything better to do, instead of doing the gardening, for example.

The golden rules which apply for the One Armed Manager that now follow have not been placed in any particular order of importance. This is a conscious choice. In order to emphasize that they are all just as important. For a better résumé for each statement a page has been reserved further along in this book.

You will notice that some items overlap each other. On one hand is that unavoidable and, at the same time, inevitable but it also underlines the importance of this subject. I have chosen to write in the masculine sense, simply out of convenience. Just so that you know.

Management is an art. No different to any other art form. The art of leaving out. Not more of this and a little of that, but *less of everything*, so that the core remains; the hard core of managing. Just as an artist or composer avoids any unnecessary frills so must a manager continually ask the question: "Does this action/interference have any added value?" or "is it really necessary for me to interfere?".

Dare therefore to trust in your personnel, accepting that some people are far more capable in doing what they get paid for than yourself (sad but true).

Hands off and allow talent to grow, take bloom and above all use, where possible, these talents. Everyone to his own; from the financial wizards to the household staff. Use them without hassling them, their knowledge, skills and talents, whilst never sitting in their chair.

Attention! Attention! That is the keyword. An iron law of management, $E = Q \times A$ effectiveness = quality x acceptance (Maiers Law) is hardly effective without a substantial dose of attention; attention promotes acceptance. Sincere interest in a sick spouse or in difficulties with the children at home will raise more loyalty than endless pep talks and bonuses.

Allow yourself to be steered by vision. Not by anything else. Know what you want and carry it out (for example via mission statements). Believe in yourself (however remain realistic and use common sense). You are not a glorified cleaner who only cleans up the mess ad hoc, and: **Choose**! You are a manager. By profession manager. Do not just do "what you are good in", but **do what you are trained for: manage** (this way you will get the best out of your personnel as well as your organisation).

For example: in the early eighties there was a tendency to name capable psychologists, (remedial) educationalists, doctors or economists on the board of directors within our healthcare organisations. Often with dramatic results: the organisation concerned more often than not lost a competent specialist and (more often than not) received a wannabe-

manager in return. Once again I therefore state:
management = a profession! Well and truly.

* Okay then, a slight slant has been added here and there.
Naturally , can you , may you (or must you sometimes) obviously
do things that you are good at, however remain critical that these
actions stand up to your mission as manager. In all other cases,
nice as a hobby but do not bother your staff with them.

Do not undertake to do what someone else can and keep your own head clear for a higher plane, the visionary aspect, the ultimate added value. Take the time to lean back in your office chair and think things over, evaluate, reflect and explore your deepest creative sources.

Be open, honest and transparent instead of perfect.
I realise it sounds neither revolutionary nor original.
Then again, just for the record.
One can create a better work of art out of a twisted branch than out of a straight plank of wood.

Both employees and management team remain the grindstone of the organisation

Conduct leadership, by pointing out the path to be followed, especially in difficult times. Show determination and willpower. Be the breaker in the surf, lead by example, and radiate tranquillity and trust. Show just that little bit more audacity and show that you, no matter what, remain confident.

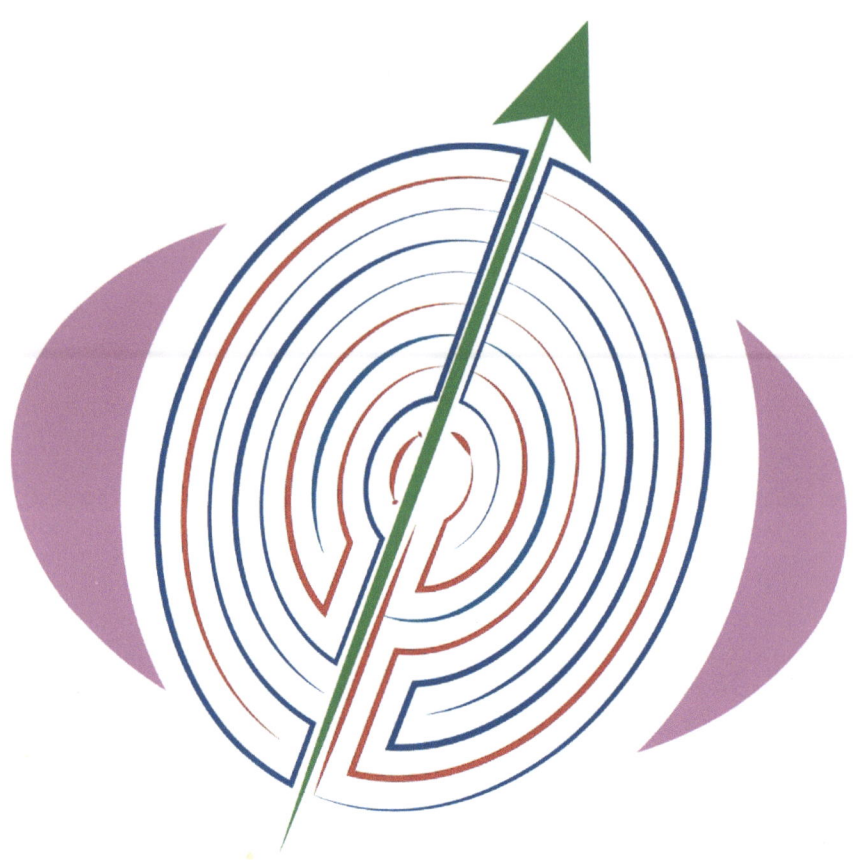

Keep it simple, at all times! Just as in this manual, no unnecessary blah blah, no exhaustive statistics or boring scientific presentations, endless shoring up, just keep to the point. Everyone is busy enough with themselves as it is. Do not go torturing your colleagues / employees with narcissistic reports, concern yourself with getting your message across plain and simple. If you like, check beforehand and see if your mother or your neighbour understands what you mean (no offence!).

The only way to get respect is to tone respect

Include your employees in brainstorming and decision-making matters in order to stimulate creativity and daring. (However you should not confuse the last with naïve solo actions or one man shows). Lay down a definite framework with visible guidelines, boundaries, authority; such as who is responsible for what. Be crucial in advance! Do however within this well defined playing area allow each player the space to show what he can and allow himself to excel therein.

Measure to make sure you know. Constantly re-evaluate your output and do not be afraid to adjust your course should you discover a slight deviation. This will not tone any instability or uncertainty, it simply testifies solely to an in depth knowledge! The world is constantly changing and with it your (potential) market.

Give employees as much chance as possible to blossom, to learn and develop (at all levels!!) and make it common practice to exchange knowledge and insights with each other without pinpointing uncommon ideas as 'weird'. Moreover, raise out-of-the-box thinking to the level of an internal art form.

Never make promises you can not keep, or where you have your doubts. It is far better to say "We are going to give this a try, give it a chance, should it not plan out we can always pull the plug if necessary". Should there be something that is simply unworkable say this without beating around the bush, even if this means upsetting certain people. Stay clearheaded! You can see more through glass than through corrugated panelling...

Communicate! Let people know what you are working on, where (if any) your doubts lie and how considerations, imaging and decision-making are progressing. Do not transpire to work with secret diaries. Mutual trust forms an important key to a successful and loyal company.

Let people know that you appreciate their
determination, knowledge and capability. Give them not
only the feeling that they are taken seriously, actually show
them that they really are of importance to the company.
Without them (their labour, interest and involvement) you
have no reason to be. None whatsoever.

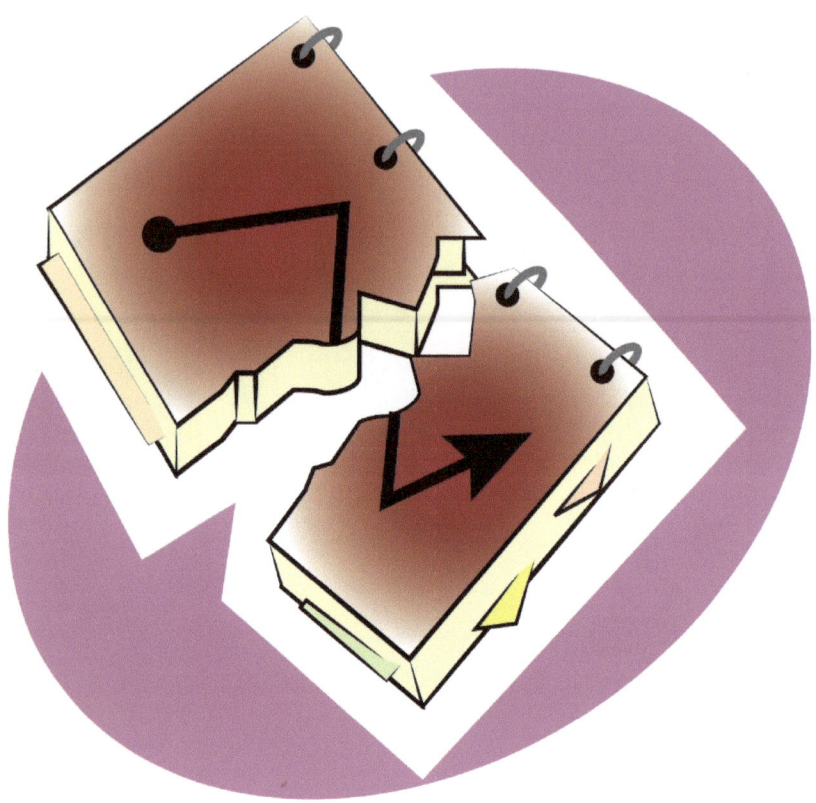

Begin reports (should these be actually necessary!) always with a summary of the essentials and most important conclusions/ recommendations. The reader can then determine himself in how far he requires to study the report. The reading of the full report may not be a requirement of every reader.

Stand up for your mistakes and stimulate your employees to do the same. Remember no one is perfect, we are surely after all human and not simply robots.

Credit where credit is due. Never take credit away from anyone else. Giving credit can be just as fulfilling

Buy **(or on occasion borrow)** a camcorder and record
yourself during a session in which you practice a
speech or are preparing an address (especially when this
has brought on an uncertain feeling in the past). You will be
amazed just how much you can benefit, in turn how much
you can learn from yourself. This will keep your head out of
the clouds and both feet firmly on the ground.

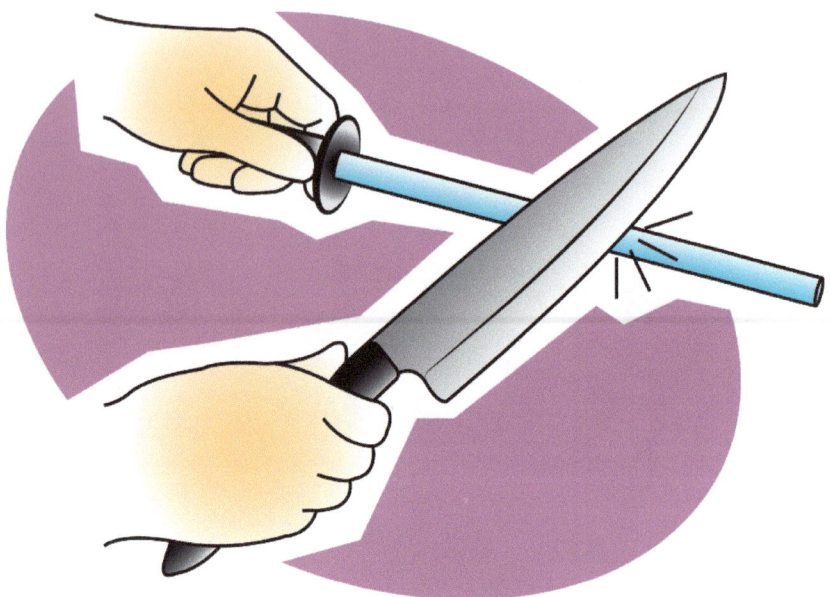

Keep each other on knife edge make the giving and receiving (of assertive) feedback the normal daily practice. Clarity leads to transparency! This above all means that everyone knows where they stand and what they can expect from each other.

Avoid the gift wrapped effect! Annoying or difficult messages which are gift wrapped to contain their meaning will, in time, have an adverse effect; this should therefore be avoided at all times. Save gift wrapping for the family at Christmas. Avoid also sentences such as "I heard that….." or "they are saying that…..".

Saying "Pete from the Logistics Dept. told me…." or "Wendy from Sales finds it tedious that…."etc, etc, sounds far better. Employees do not need to have to guess who said what, or where a rumour and hearsay are brought into the world. This creates trust and chokes off any gossip before it gets started.
Everyone is then able to look his colleagues straight in the eye and any criticism will not be undermined but substantiated.

Wave off any vague insinuations and be wary that you do not use them yourself.

A board hung in the foyer with the text "*Be Specific Or Be Quiet*" will get over your message from the off, make this statement an interim part of your companies policy.

Tolerance will lead to chaos. Anything that can not be tolerated should simply not be accepted. View nothing through veiled fingers but take a clear and concise view and on no occasion should you allow anything to cloud your judgement out of sympathy This kind of practise will lead to the beginning of the end.

Do not trifle or politicise! Should the water be up to the lips of everyone else acknowledge this immediately, take things from there. You need not allow yourself to be caught up or bogged down in other people's negativity and pessimism, but on the other hand you must take your business seriously and not allow euphemisms and understatements to take control. Nothing is more frustrating for hard working employees than to have to listen to academic twaddle which is only aimed at removing any fears and displeasures. When the dog has died, say so instead of "he is not feeling all that well at the moment".

*One straw too many will break the camels
back!
(or: if you push too hard....)*

Every action = a statement! Be very aware of this! You are a manager, someone who never just does this or that but plans ahead. Always.

Ensure that all expectations (in both directions) are **clear and concise**: What do you expect from your employees? What are we aiming for? What are our goals and targets? How do we treat our colleagues and clients? A clear and binding mission statement will help and support us in our work, just take care not to attempt to replace the bible, rather a handy compass.

Remember that nothing changes more than our own society, our organisation is herein no different. (Do not get involved with every new hype and fashion, ensure that your profile remains focused: this is what we are good at, better than our competitors, acknowledge that no one can achieve everything and leave the specialized work to the specialized companies).

Specializing against presenting us to the world/taking our position.

Remain upstanding for your aims without becoming **rigid, ensuring that enough flexibility remains** in order to follow new avenues of chance, at the same time adapting to any and all threats and demands evolving from this ever changing society (The eternal dilemma of which choice to take, -in fact- the manager's paradox).

Be distinct when presenting bad news, come straight to the point. Do not attempt any cover up, stick strictly to the facts. Do not belittle (in advance) any reaction from an employee. If blood needs to be drawn then pain will be felt. Give everyone the chance to air their feelings and misgivings as long as these remain constructive. It is not the intention to mire people down. Highlight all and any positive points giving further directions leading to a solution, this gives an insight into what is to follow. Always close on a positive note. Show that at the end of every dark tunnel light is to be found.

Take every day at least one hour sabbatical

Should you as a manager be unsure in a certain situation, do not just act as though you know what you are doing. Be honest to others and yourself, saying "sorry, not right sure at the moment, would you lend me a hand please" will make you not only more human as a manager in the eyes of others, but will also empower the skills, professionalism and loyalty of those who surround you. They will then realise that they are not just taken for granted. Their input is viewed to be just as important as that of everyone else.

Remember to radiate trust that a positive conclusion will be reached. Should you as a manager not emit this we shall overcome this together, then can your cry for help be interpreted as a panic manoeuvre and work adversely, raising the question: has he lost the clue, oh no! What now?

Dare to trust in your own intuition. In fact, cherish this as this is what makes you as a manager unique. Not every decision or action (whether taken before or seen with hindsight) can be viewed to have been carefully calculated, nor is this necessary.

Was this the case then it would surely be simple to exchange you for someone –anyone- who had taken the time out to follow one of the many management courses which are currently available...

Should you not have the feeling for something or not understand it, do not just act as though you do. This will make yourself and your work as a manager impossible. It is better to say "No matter what, I still do not have a good feeling about this" or if you prefer "I am not able to follow this at the moment" .This way you will remain believable and keep your credibility.

W **atch your conduct!** Focus not only on your literal, also your physical appearance, but also on the way you project yourself. Away from your knowledge and skills as a manager your conduct and becoming are an important measure of how you bring your beliefs over to others. Look after yourself, walk upright, talk calmly, distinctly, be courteous whilst taking care to make enough eye contact. An open door you may think? Well take the time to look around you to see exactly what is going on…

Realise at all times in everything that you do and project that you are the manager, the person who walks up front, the one that sticks his neck out first. Do not act out the "city gent", save that for the bar when you are among friends.

* Forget all about "primus inter pares" garbage. Do you have the same rights among equals? Or are you just a little more equal than the others (as in Orwell's book)? Should you enjoy endlessly philosophizing on this subject that is your prerogative and you should do so, however as long as you are the one behind the managers desk you are not equal: you are the leader, the person who determines the course to be set and monitors this, end of subject.

It shows far more genius to be able to turn an upmost complicated subject into something that is simple to deduce, easy to follow instead of intellectualising standard issues into an incomprehensible mush. De latter testifies solely to a vain ego trip

Management & opportunism: many (young) managers have an opportunistic attitude and tend to shop around in management land in search of what is on offer. In principle there is nothing wrong with this, however ensure that you lay down a solid base on which your successor can build. Being a job hopper is one thing, leaving behind an unwanted unmanageable mess, with the attitude of 'not my problem anymore, let the next one work it out' (having also the audacity to let yourself be bought out due to non-performance with a golden handshake!) is unworthy of any respectable manager.

Finally here are several recurring misconceptions; **leadership and managing are not synonymous of each other** although they do go hand in hand. One good example of leadership *without managing* is - as far as I am concerned- Gordon Ramsay in his series "Hell's Kitchen". He tones leadership whilst at times appearing almost as a coach. This cultivates, due to his bullish attitude and total lack of respect, more turmoil, envy, distrust, opposition and personal planning. It is possible that Ramsay has no intention to act the role of manager, this however is a poor excuse but does not account for his performance. Let it be patently obvious that no manager will benefit from this kind of attitude towards his employees, on the contrary.

The second and also last misconception that I would like to bring to your attention is **the difference between being relentless and ruthless**. You are relentless whenever and wherever you require to be to get the job done, in other words you do not pull on kid's gloves when delivering your message, remaining always calm and lucid. You are a manager with a heart. Ruthless however is something completely different, you are no longer concerned with the feelings of the recipient of your message, (often viewed that you actually take pleasure out of inflicting hurt upon others). This kind of vulgarity has no home in the house of a manager.

At least one hand of the One Armed Manager is repeatedly to be found in his trouser pocket, both of his legs however are planted firmly on the ground; his right leg being the strong financial person whilst his left is a talented, proactive secretary. Should this not be so then can be concluded that he is shackled dragging a lead weight with him on both legs....

IN CLOSING

A dermatologist who happens to be a good friend of mine suggested to me to use the title for this reading matter, "Tips and Tricks for managers". I forgave him.... The readers who acknowledge the essence of this book, understanding its intentions will understand exactly as to why I chose not to use that title. Wanting to use the term 'tips' is conceivable however the term 'tricks' is completely out of context. A manager who interprets these golden One Armed rules as tricks has completely missed the point and is more suited to a role in the circus where he would not be out of place as an illusionist.

I sincerely hope that this short sketch has helped lift the edge of the veil which hangs over what in essence is *the Art of Managing*. That it has become clear that managing is more than abstract leadership or just coaching (a somewhat blurred term that should be avoided at all times). You would be astounded of the number of (who appertain to be) experienced 'managers' that falsely refer to themselves as a 'manager' doing causing untold damage to our profession – likewise wrongly- giving us a bad name. Whereby, not wanting to repeat myself, but this does need to be said: this is and always will be a specialised trade, I would even go so far as saying one of the finest! Let us all take care that it stays this way....

Here's hoping that you all find pleasure in your work as a One Armed Manager, your colleague, Morcqx.